This Has to be a Lie...

Tareasha Mon'ea

Copyright © 2023 Taresha Mon'ea
All rights reserved.
ISBN: 9798397004633

No part of this publication may be reproduced, distributed, or transmitted in any form, including photocopying, recording, or other electronic or mechanical methods, without the prior written permission of the author, except in the case of brief quotations embodied in critical reviews and certain other noncommercial uses permitted by copyright law.

Although the author and publisher have made every effort to ensure that the information in this book was correct at press time, the author and publisher do not assume and hereby disclaim any liability to any party for any loss, damage, or disruption caused by errors or omissions, whether such errors or omissions result from negligence, accident, or any other cause.

Scripture quotations marked NKJV are taken from The Holy Bible, New King James Version ®. New King James Version is a registered trademark of Crossway ®.

Thank You

This book is dedicated to my beloved parents, Carl and Carolyn Davis. Your love and support these 40 years are what keeps me going. I love you!

A special thanks to THEE Justin O. Ruffin, wheeeeeeeeeeeeew it's been a long time coming, right? For your pour, for your prayers, for listening to me ramble, vent, understanding my tears and always being a safe place. You are indeed MY brother and friend. This would not be possible without you!

I'd also like to acknowledge my mentor and sister, Rebecca (Michael-Elliot) Rice. You (both) have walked through this journey of healing with me and were not afraid of all of my mess, to challenge me, to correct me and most importantly love me to this place of wholeness. THANK YOU!

Thank you to every person that has poured into me in any capacity on this journey.

THIS HAS TO BE A LIE…

Table of Contents

Introduction 1
Day 1: 5
Day 2: 8
Day 3: 11
Day 4: 14
Day 5: 17
Day 6: 21
Day 7: 24
Day 8: 27
Day 9: 30
Day 10: 34
Day 11: 37
Day 12: 40
Day 13: 43
Day 14: 47
Day 15: 50
Day 16: 53
Day 17: 56
Day 18: 59
Day 19: 62

Day 20: 65

Day 21: 68

About the Author 70

Introduction

Whew! I can't believe I did this! I can't believe this is finally complete. This book is a...so many things. It is a testimony that I'm still here. It is a sign that there is more for me (and you). It is a symbol of the fact that my heart is still beating and pumping through all I've endured. It is a sign that I survived. It is a small preview of my journey to wholeness. To be honest, I have started and stopped this journey many times. Each attempt began with a clear destination, but along the way the work required somehow, sometimes, made the once clear destination foggier. Although, my journey is not yet complete, I wanted to share 21 affirmations that have helped me along the way, with you.

It took 21 days to create a habit and I found this to be true. No matter how many times I seemed to stop and start this journey, one thing I stuck with (or that stuck with me) was affirmations. Some of these I recited daily, and others have become a part of my life. Changing your mindset is key to completing any journey and this was no different for me. It is my prayer that the next 21 days serve as a catalyst in helping you start the process you've been overthinking or just flat out choosing not to start.

I don't want to lie to you and say that this will be easy; some days it won't be. I don't want you to believe that your life will take some magical 180 degree turn and look different than it does now, once this is over. I don't want to sell you false hope. However, what I want to do is tell you what you can expect because I lived it.

Expect to cry. There will be days when the process of healing and wholeness becomes unbearable. There will be days when you will reconsider what you're doing and why you're doing it. There will be days when you quit the process, and that's okay. When you finish crying, wipe your eyes, get up, and get back into the fight.

Expect to see things and people differently. As your eyes are opened and the lies you believed are exposed, you will see things you didn't see before. The lenses of your rose-colored glasses will shatter and what you see on the other side will not always be pretty. Red flags that you overlooked (intentionally or otherwise) will be shown and you will have to make tough decisions. Feel the pain, sober yourself, and do what you must do. Remember, your life (heart, mind, soul, and body) is at stake.

Expect to heal. One thing we know about healing is that it is painful at times. When you break a limb, sometimes they must be rebroken to ensure that they heal properly. In the same way, as you go through this journey, you may find yourself being rebroken. Expect to experience pain, but anticipate the healing that will come on the other side. Be committed to yourself and the process and you will be just fine.

THIS HAS TO BE A LIE…

Day 1:

I am enough, Period!

I am enough, right? This is something I struggle(d) to believe. From my upbringing to various toxic relationships, experiencing heartbreak, losing friends, church transition, and many other experiences I questioned my enough-ness (no, that's not a real word, but that's okay) often. I found myself questioning my value more times than I am willing to admit or able to count. Being in spaces that do not value you can sometimes cause you to doubt yourself. It can take a toll on your mental, emotional, physical, and spiritual health. And that's what it did for me.

In the midst of these experiences, I would find myself giving myself pep talks. I don't know when or how they started, but I would say things like, "Tareasha, you can do this. All that matters is that you know your heart. I know what my intention was, and no one can tell me anything different." And even though I would say these things, I didn't always believe it. These statements would often be followed by a series of questions like, "What did I do wrong? What can I fix next time around? How can I be better?". Now, the truth of the matter is there is nothing wrong with improvement. However, the challenge comes when you feel that you have to improve because you aren't good enough as you are.

I believe the lie that I wasn't worthy of love and that I'd never find it. I believed that my family would never be whole. I believed that I was doing something wrong when the reality is, it wasn't [always] me. Now, I agree and align with the truth. The truth is that my best is enough. I am far from perfect, but I am being perfected every day. I am enough, just as I am, and I don't have to change anything for anyone but me. I am enough. Period!

Reflection: Have you ever felt that you weren't enough? Do you feel that way now?

Write an affirmation that you will say to yourself whenever you or someone questions you or makes you feel that you are not enough.

_____
_____
_____
_____
_____
_____
_____

Day 2:

Good things are happening to me every day, and I notice them.

When life is happening, it can be a difficult feat to remain (or be) optimistic. It can be equally challenging to step outside of what you may be experiencing to notice that in the midst of the bad things that are prevalent and taking place, that there is some good in there too. In order to see it, though, you must change your perspective. You have to choose to see the good and embrace it. You have to find the silver lining and hold on to that.

Good things are happening to you every day. In spite of the negativity, you see on the news, social media, or your family group chat there are good things happening every day. You just have to be intentional about seeing them. Even when bad things happen, it shouldn't define your life or your day. You have to learn to see or find the good in everything.

Noticing the good requires you to recognize that every negative thing you experience in life serves a purpose. You must see these moments as opportunities for growth and change, rather than defeat and depression. I used to believe the lie that nothing was going right for me. I believed that the cycles of disappointment, grief, pain, and loss would last forever. I couldn't see beyond what was in my face, so it was hard to believe anything else. Now, I know the truth. The truth is that nothing bad lasts forever. My good days outweigh my bad days, and I have whatever it takes to make it through the obstacles in my life. Good things are happening around me and to me. I just have to take the time to recognize it.

Reflection: What are you experiencing that you are finding difficult to find the good in? Identify three good things that are present in that situation and be intentional about being grateful for them every day! After you identify those things, write your own affirmation that you will speak over yourself when you need to hear it most.

_____

_____

_____

_____

_____

_____

_____

Day 3:

No matter what I've done or what happened to me. I deserve to still excel and succeed! I deserve to heal. I deserve to have joy. I deserve to have peace. I deserve to thrive and not just survive, I deserve happiness! Nothing disqualifies me from that.
~ Terrell Pressley

Life has a funny way of impacting our thoughts and the way we see ourselves. When you are constantly a part of cycles that leave you on the short end of the stick, it is hard to believe that there is anything better…or that anything different is something you truly deserve. One thing I have had to constantly remind myself of, while on this journey, is that I don't have to settle for anything less than what *I* deem as worthy or acceptable for my life.

Growing up in an African American family, I was sometimes made to feel, as if what I desired did not matter. Some of us were born into situations that activated our fight or flight sense. We were in survival mode before we even recognized what it was and by the time we did, we were too far gone. The hope of living a peaceful life seemed to be a distant reality; but it doesn't have to be that way. When you recognize that what you have been given is not what you deserve it ignites a hunger in you to search for what satisfies you. It pushes you to evaluate relationships on every level and set boundaries, disengage, or show up differently in those spaces. The key to walking in this level of freedom is not found in other people; it comes from within. Only you can set the bar for what you deserve and when you say it don't allow others to enter your life without meeting that standard.

I fell for the lie that said I had to take what was given to me. I had to endure poor treatment because it was the best someone else could do. I had to be okay with being treated unfairly and overlooked. Not so! I know the truth now. The truth is that if someone's best is not on my level, I don't have to accept it. I can honor it, but I don't have to allow it into my space. I am not what happened to me. I am only what I say, and I am and who I purpose in my heart to me. That is the truth!

Reflection: What have you experienced that made you feel like you didn't deserve to grow or elevate? Maybe you're going through something like that right now. Create an affirmation to remind yourself that you deserve to live a life that is full of the good things you desire.

_____

_____

_____

_____

_____

Day 4:

I already have it all, What I don't see with my eyes is growing in my heart. expressed in my dreams & on its way to my reality,
~ David McGraw

I know it may be hard to believe but everything you desire in life is already in your possession. While you may look at your life and believe this is a lie, I want to share my perspective with you. Every skill, talent, and level of passion and pursuit that you need to accomplish your dreams is already in you. If it wasn't, your dreams wouldn't be what they are. What is lacking is your internal realization that you are not without what you need to be successful. You are also not without the ability to create a plan to achieve or obtain it.

Having it all must be defined for each of us, and when you define that you may realize that the things you thought you needed were actually things that didn't come from you. Maybe they came from your family or your friend group. It may come from what you see on social media or on TV. But what does your version of "having it all" look like? Could it be that you have been going after things that you really don't need to satisfy you, or have you been rejecting what you need to find your happiness? I know it may sound crazy, but I want you to believe that you already have everything you need within you. Look at your skills, embrace your talents, reflect on what you have survived, and know that it is that determination and resilience that will carry you to your dreams.

I used to believe the lie that I had to settle or compromise in one area of my life or another just to be happy. I believed I could only have part of my "all" instead of the total portion. I believe that I had to settle because it "all" would never be available to or for me. Now, I believe that I can [and will] have everything I want in this life. Although it may take some time for me to get there, I will continue this journey and I will not settle until "all" the things in my life come into alignment and my dreams come into fruition.

Reflection: What does having it all look like to you? Are you struggling to believe you can have it all? Create an affirmation that will encourage you to pursue all that you desire, and post is somewhere visible so you can read it when you start to question the process.

_____

_____

_____

_____

_____

_____

_____

Day 5:

I can do all things through things through Christ who gives me strength
-Philippians 4:13 (NKJV)

This scripture is one that I learned when I was younger, but it is something that I apply to my life every day. When I think about what this really means, I have to understand that this does not solely apply to supernatural feats, big projects, and working to become a millionaire. I have to understand that included under the umbrella of "all things" is the ability to get out of bed to do what I have to do in a day. When we begin to think about doing *all* things through Christ, I wonder if we apply this verse to the smaller things in the same way that we do the bigger things we want to accomplish.

Because of some of the things that I experienced, I often felt as if I did not have anything left to give – to myself or to others.

It was in those moments that I had to rely on the strength of the Lord to make it through. There were days that leaving my house seemed to be too daunting of a task. Other days I didn't have the physical energy to go to work. There were times when I would sit in the car for hours, thinking about all that was going wrong in my life. On this journey, this scripture meant more to me than what I could accomplish; it became an encouragement and reminded me of the fact that the things that seemed so difficult, that some people take for granted, were also possible for me.

I know some days may be harder than others, but those are the times where you will need to be reminded of this even more. There is nothing you cannot do, but you must learn to do it in the strength of the Lord. Let Him be strong for you when you cannot be strong for yourself. And in these moments, don't try to be strong for other people. Be honest about where you are and what you are able to do. You will be better because of it... and a better you is the ultimate goal.

I believed the lie that I had to work hard to do things on my own. Being let down has a way of pushing you to be so independent that you forget to even turn to God for help. Have you been there? Now I walk in what I call strong weakness. I am honest about my weakness because that when God gives me the strength I need (2 Corinthians 12:9). I no longer lie about being the strong friend, because somedays I'm not strong, friend.

Reflection: What have you been trying to accomplish in your own strength? What have you been removing from your "all things" list? Take some time to ask God to give you strength to do what is required of you. Write an affirmation that you will use when you need more strength to get things done.

_____

_____

_____

THIS HAS TO BE A LIE…

Day 6:

All things work for my good, always,

Life...it be life-ing these days. If you're reading this, I'm sure you can agree. There are times that the darkness that comes as a byproduct of situations makes us believe that nothing good is happening for us and that nothing good will come of the work that we are putting in. If I'm honest, there are times where I wanted to give up because it just didn't seem worth it to try anymore. It didn't seem worth it to work and pay bills and not have any money. It didn't seem worth it to date and end up with the same kind of guy who wasn't about anything and didn't want anything more than temporary fun. It didn't seem worth it to live. In those moments, I felt like it would be easier to end it all.

What I had to realize was that although I could not see it, that there were great things happening behind the scenes, or just beyond what I could see. When I changed my perspective, I learned to see and extract the good out of these negative situations. I learned that these failed relationships were teaching me boundaries and showing me what I did not want. I learned that trying was proof of my resilience. I learned that my job wasn't going to meet all of my needs and I discovered dormant gifts and abilities that I needed to tap into. It was in this process (and it was a long process) that I realized that although life was happening good things were happening as well. I wasn't a victim, but I was put in a position to discover new things. Do not fall for the lie that says nothing good will happen to you. The truth is that good things will always happen to you; you just have to be willing to see them.

Reflection: Can you believe that all the things you have experienced, and are experiencing, are working for your good? I know it's hard to think about, but settle in that. You must be intentional about seeing the good. Create an affirmation that will help you take note of the good regardless of the bad that may be happening in your life.

_____
_____
_____
_____
_____
_____
_____

Day 7:

I'm exactly where I'm supposed to be right now.

When I was in high school, there was a lot of emphasis placed on knowing what I wanted to do after I graduated. We spent time taking aptitude tests, going on college tours, and being told that after graduation life would change, we would officially be adults, and a part of the "real world". As I participated in these events, I created a version of my future that wasn't completely realistic. There were things that I wanted then that I'm grateful that I never received. On the other side, there are also things that I wanted then that I am still longing for. My five- and 10-year plans have been chopped, altered, and reconstructed many times. When I look at what remains sometimes it feels like I'm behind.

This feeling of being behind often times comes from comparison. When we look at the lives of younger individuals, who have "accomplished more" than we have, or we see our peers going to do and have the things we desire, it opens the door for feelings of inadequacy to set in. We compare our lives to those around us, almost subconsciously, and the result of that comparison often leaves us depressed and unmotivated.

I planned, often times, what my life should look like by the age of 40. I figured by now, I'd have a husband, children, and be living some version of my ideal life. I didn't imagine that I'd be healing from past trauma, fighting daily for my mental health, becoming a champion of mental health, and writing a book about my struggles. This is not what I planned. In fact, if you would've told me, when I was in high school, that I would be here, I would say "this has to be a lie." But it is true. I may not have all the things that I desire, but I refuse to settle for the lie that says I am behind. I am exactly where I need to be at this moment, and the things that I am experiencing in this moment or preparing me for what I desire. My desires are changing, my mind is evolving, my heart is being mended, so that when I receive what I have been praying for I will be able to do so, without fear, hesitation, or restriction. The truth is that you are not behind schedule. Regardless of how it feels, you are right on time.

Reflection: Comparison comes to rob you of your gratitude. It influences feelings of envy and causes you to feel that you are inadequate. You are exactly where you should be right now. Rest in that! Write an affirmation that you will carry with you to ground you in the moment and help you focus on *your* journey.

_____

_____

_____

_____

_____

Day 8:

I do what is best for me even when that is difficult.

In 2022, I made one of the hardest decisions of my life. After six years, I made the decision to leave my job for the sake of my mental health. This was something that I never would've imagined that I would have to do, but it was necessary. For almost a year, I found myself in and out of urgent care, emergency rooms, and admitted to the hospital. The stress of my position was taking a toll on me physically, and the symptoms were debilitating at times.

From headaches to chest pains or difficulty breathing, I spent so much time in the hospital, not knowing what the problem was. I was emotionally eating, which caused weight gain and that was not the best thing for me. Before I made the decision to leave, I had gone up for promotion and was denied several times for no reason. My supervisors and managers found everything they could and used it as a reason to keep me in my current role, even though they knew I was qualified for the position and able to do it. This was a very dark time for me, and for a while I couldn't see my way out.

I believed the lie that said, "if I work hard enough, everything will be OK". I believed that if I performed well that I would be promoted. And while this is true, it is not always the case. That year, I made a decision to take a drastic pay cut to ensure that I was mentally healthy and able to be there for myself and my tribe. This was not easy, but it was a less stressful ride. Although it was difficult, I had to do what was best for me, and I don't regret it at all. My new position has allowed me to relaunch my business and establish myself as an entrepreneur. This is what living my best life looks like. What does that look like to you?

Reflection: What does your best life look like? Write an affirmation that you will give you the courage to do what's best even when things get difficult.

Day 9:

I will celebrate every win - big or small.
- Justin Foster

Over the years I have watched many individuals, myself included, struggle to celebrate themselves. We grow up and become a part of spaces that teach us the value of honoring and celebrating others, but we are rarely taught or shown how to honor ourselves. Instead of self-celebration being a common occurrence, it has become a novelty of some sort. It becomes something that we do when we accomplish "big" milestones, but we often overlook the "smaller" things that we accomplish. We diminish the effort that it took to accomplish or obtain the goal and move on to the next thing.

One thing that I had to practice, and sometimes still struggle with, was celebrating every moment of my journey. Every goal I accomplish, and the steps I take toward that goal should be celebrated. Now, I'm not talking about having pointless celebrations to acknowledge frivolous things; but I'm talking about acknowledging the effort that you put into making things happen. The hard work, dedication, and commitment that it takes to work toward your goals every day should be recognized. You shouldn't have to wait for your birthday or until you finish your degree, you can celebrate passing a difficult class or acknowledging the fact that you've gone one month with no soda. When you know how deeply you struggle with something, making improvements in that area should be celebrated.

Another thing I had to do to adopt the practice is removing the term "small" from my vocabulary as a relates to my victories. There are no small victories. Everything I do is big because it took work. I celebrate my wins because I don't want to fall back in the habit of waiting for others to do it, and being in my feelings when they don't. I celebrate my wins because my accomplishments matter. I celebrate my wins because they are my wins.

I believed the lies that said, celebrating myself was pride and wasn't a good look. Now, I walk with the truth that celebrating myself is pride, and I am proud of everything I accomplish today, I hope you divorce yourself from the "small win" mentality and celebrate everything you accomplish. Treat yourself to a spa day or buy a new journal. Whatever you do, celebrate the work you put in. It's necessary!

Reflection: As you take time to think about what you've accomplished, create an affirmation that you will use to remind you to celebrate what you accomplish! It ain't nothing small about it.

_____

_____

TAREASHA MON'EA

Day 10:

I am not the mistakes I've made,

One of the most challenging obstacles on my healing journey was (and is) people. There were times that I wished I didn't have to deal with them or be around them, but life isn't life without people. A lesson I learned about people is that they can be unforgiving. They take the mistakes of your past and hold them against you forever. They rejoice in your poor decisions and make you feel as if you're a prisoner to the mistakes of your past. Maybe you've experienced this or maybe you've been part of the reason that someone else has. It's like the one time you make a mistake it becomes a part of your identity.

If you are reading this, and you have been in this place or you're currently there, I want you to know that you are not defined by your mistakes. Yes, you made some wrong decisions. Yes, you made some plans that didn't quite work out. Yes, people may have been hurt by the things you did, or did not do; but that does not define you. What defines you is your resilience, your love, your passion, and your ability to never stop dreaming. What defines you is you taking responsibility for the things you have done and working to correct them. This does not mean that you should live a lifetime feeling indebted to those that were impacted by your choices; but it does mean that you should spend the rest of your life working to become a better version of yourself.

The lie about a mistake says that you'll never be more than that. The truth of the matter is, you were always more than that. Temporary lapses in judgment, making decisions with limited resources, and doing what you felt was best while you were in survival mode is not a condemnable act... it is an act of bravery, and I want you to see them as such. You may have made some mistakes, and you will make more; but I want you to learn from them and keep going.

Reflection: Yes, it happened. Yes, you did it. Yes, it's over! You can't change the past, but you can move forward. Write an affirmation that will empower you to move beyond your mistakes and move toward greater.

_____
_____
_____
_____
_____
_____
_____

Day 11:

I am embracing my potential to be, do and have whatever I desire,

Potential... Where do we begin? If you are a part of pop culture, in any way, shape or form, then you know there is much debate about potential. Should potential be acknowledged, or ignored: that is the question. Often times, I hear people say that they are no longer settling for potential, they are only going for things that are concrete. While I understand where they are coming from, I disagree with that sentiment. To ignore potential, and only focus on what is present, often illuminates the possibility of what can be. Whenever you are in a situation where possibility is limited, you'll find yourself walking in darkness. And when you find yourself walking in darkness, your current state becomes your grave.

When it came to this healing journey, I had to recognize that potential was not something to be feared, but it was a space to be filled. I also had to recognize that I had what it took to fill that space. My dreams, aspirations, hopes, and desires, which have not been realized, are potential outcomes. However, it is the work that I put in (or do not put in) today that determines whether or not that potential will be realized, and *how* it will be realized. I used to believe the lies that said potential wasn't worth anything, but now I know that all great things start with potential. I had to embrace my potential to "be," which created room and space for me to grow and become. Don't discount a thing, because of potential, rather ask whether or not there is a plan to become.

Reflection: Potential is necessary. That's it; that's the post. Create an affirmation that will highlight your potential and encourage you to fill the space until it no longer exists.

_____

_____

TAREASHA MON'EA

Day 12:

I take this moment to release anything I am carrying that is too heavy to level up,

As adults we often pride ourselves on being able to carry multiple things. Adulting has become about juggling the various responsibilities of our day-to-day lives, and seemingly doing it without frustration or being overwhelmed. Although this is a goal for many people, it is often not possible. We do not go through life untouched by the things we experience. Also, we hold the things that we experience in various ways. Some of us hold experiences in our bodies and they show up in the form of tension, pain, aches, and other physical ailments. Others of us hold them in our minds, and they manifest in the form of negative thoughts, overthinking, and varying levels of paranoia. And others hold these experiences in our emotions, causing us to lash out or experience things like depression or other mental health disorders.

I believed the lie that said, I had to take everything in stride, never speak up or out about what happened to me and keep things bottled up. Now, I walk with the truth that I don't have to carry everything that I have experienced. I learned to practice meditation and be intentional about actively releasing any negativity or trauma that I was carrying based on what I endured. In the middle of my most overwhelming and frustrating moments, I had to stop and practice the art of releasing and that is something I want you to do as you're reading this.

Think of the things that are bothering you, frustrating you, or causing you to feel overwhelmed. Rather than working on a solution at this moment, I want you to release those feelings because they are too heavy for you. As you lighten your load, you will be free to be, and handle situations with a clear head, heart, and spirit. Don't believe the lie, but walk in truth and take this moment to release anything that is too heavy so you can move forward and level up.

Reflection: Write an affirmation that speaks to what you are releasing and what you are accepting in its place.

_____
_____
_____
_____
_____
_____
_____

Day 13:

I'm finding new ways to love myself, I try my best to treat myself well, I release thoughts that bring me down, I accept energy and ideas that light me up, Self-love flows through my body, I'm healing every day and that makes me happy,
-Sylvester McNutt II

In the words of Rihanna, "we all want love." What I've come to recognize on this journey to wholeness is that love is everything, but it has to start with self, first. Many of us desire to be loved by other people, but I think we fail to truly love ourselves first. And old adage says, "if you don't love yourself, how the hell can you love someone else?" And that is a question that many individuals have yet to answer. One of the most paramount lessons I learned was loving myself...more specifically, loving myself in new (different) ways based on what I was going through.

In the same way, that love can look different for the people that are part of our lives, it can also look different for us based on the seasons that we're in or the situations we may be facing. In some seasons, loving myself, looked like beating my face to go nowhere. In other seasons, it looked like eating crab legs with my girls. In some moments, it was retail therapy and spa days that were needed. Flowers, quiet (or loud) nights at home, or being with family were all things I did as a sign that I loved. Although some of these events involved other people, that was OK because I was in control of what I wanted to do, and I did just that.

I didn't feel pressured to hang out with people if I didn't want to. I didn't feel like I was less than a friend, sister, daughter, or any of the other titles that I hold, because

I wanted to be by myself. I also didn't see myself in a negative light because I wanted to be around others. Doing what I wanted to do to make me happy was what I needed, and I did that without apology.

I believed the lie that said, I needed to have people in my life to be loved, and to feel loved. The truth of the matter is as long as I love myself that's enough. As people, we are relational beings, so I don't want to promote this one-woman (man) show. However, I do want to promote a show that goes on, even if no one is in the audience. Dance like no one's watching, get dolled up to sit in your living room. Show yourself that you love yourself and when that standard is set others will follow.

Reflection: What does loving yourself look like? Create an affirmation that speaks to finding the freedom to love yourself unapologetically.

_____

_____

_____

THIS HAS TO BE A LIE…

_____
_____
_____
_____

Day 14:

You've got to pour that same love into yourself that you give away so freely. You can't be of service to others if you aren't a service to yourself.

Growing up in an African American family, I was taught to be selfless and to give to others. Being a Christian, that same principle was reinforced. While I won't blame anybody for the way I practiced this principle, I will admit that I did find a lot of error with the way that this was presented to me. Yes, we should be selfless, and we should be willing to give love to others, but that love shouldn't come with some of the hefty prices that we have, and may currently be paying. Our lives are too valuable to give without receiving and they are too valuable to give without honoring what is being given.

So, think about what you do for others. When was the last time you did those same things for yourself? I'm not talking about doing the exact same thing because you may not need what they need; I'm talking about the level of effort, passion, and determination you exert when making things happen for other people. When was the last time you made yourself a priority? Do you even know what that feels like?

I believed the lie that said I was a better person if I put myself last, and always gave myself the short end of the stick. I believed that as long as I was integral that the Lord would repay people for how they mistreated me. Although that is true, I also recognize that He gave me the power to enforce boundaries and that was what I did. The truth is, I can't be good to or for anyone else if I'm not good to myself. The greater truth is, I am worth being good to myself and that is not negotiable.

Reflection: Loving yourself is a skill you must master. Failing to do so will result in your being unable to effectively love others. Write an affirmation about self-love that you will apply daily.

_____
_____
_____
_____
_____

Day 15:

I am surrounded by love and abundance.

Everyone wants to be around people who have good vibes and good energy. No one wants to constantly be around a Debbie downer or someone who is constantly complaining. At one point, that was me. I couldn't see the good that was happening around me because of all the bad stuff that was happening *to* me. I could not see beyond my current circumstance and allow hope to rise within. One day I had to stop, take a step back and recognize that, although I may not have always been able to see it (because of what I was focused on), I was surrounded by love and abundance.

This is not a cliché or some fluffy affirmation that creates a world full of delusion. It is a reality. Every day you are surrounded by people who want the best for you, who will challenge you, and will not let you settle. You are surrounded by an abundance of positivity, creativity, wisdom, joy, peace, and light that God gives every one of us. You are surrounded by signs that encourage you to keep going, even when you want to quit. You are surrounded by individuals who see you for who you are and love you authentically.

The lie says that there is nothing good happening to or around you. It dictates that things will never get or be any better than they are now. The picture painted by the lie is one that says that you will always be in a place of lack and you won't know or embrace true love. The truth is that love is already around you. It is near you even when you can't sense it. The truth is that you will come out of everything you are in, and you will be better because of what you went through. You don't have to settle for the lie, but if you want to see the truth you must push for it. It's just on the other side of what's in front of you.

Reflection: When you are feeling void of love and care you are not your best. Write an affirmation that you will use when you need to be reminded of the love and abundance that surrounds you.

_____

_____

_____

_____

_____

_____

_____

Day 16:

I have good days and bad days, Both are ok.

If you've grown up in church or been to a black funeral, then you've probably heard the song "I won't complain". The song starts out like this, "I've had some good days, I've had some hills to climb. I've had some weary days. And some sleepless nights...". This song is very true. Although this song is full of complaints, the essence of this song says that every day won't be good, but every day won't be bad. Whatever day you may find yourself having it is OK. Everything around us tells us that we must live lives of perfection and become people that don't have negativity in their lives; but that is a lie...flat out!

I remember when the smallest hiccup to my plans or interruption to my routine would throw my entire day off. Depending on what happened, it was oftentimes hard to rebound, and I usually wouldn't be able to reset or recover until the following day. When I think about the amount of time I spent focusing on things that I could not change, it's almost embarrassing. I believed that my life had to be perfect and if I lived a perfect life, then I would be perfect too. But that was a lie.

The truth is that we will have bad days, but there is always good to be found in the bad. Every storm has a silver lining and even though we don't like rain it has a purpose. It's OK to have good days and it's OK to have bad days. The key is taking on the lessons that are presented to you and learning everything there is to learn from them.

Reflection: Bad days will come, but the good will always come behind them. In the space below, write an affirmation that will help you endure bad days.

_____
_____
_____

TAREASHA MON'EA

Day 17:

I am the only person responsible for my happiness and my life, I need to take charge of it now.

In 2019, Will Smith received a lot of flak, on social media, for a statement he made in an interview. During that interview, he mentioned that his wife's happiness was not his responsibility, and people were in a bit of an uproar. The comments in response to that were varied, but I found what he said to be true. No one in this world is responsible for your happiness but you. When we recognize this, I think we will find more happy people. Relying on others to be the sole source of our happiness puts us at their mercy and removes the power that we have in our own lives. Putting that much responsibility on others is unfair to them, but it is also unfair to you. Choosing to be lazy so others can make you happy indicates that you might not truly want to be happy.

There was a time in my life where I believed that my happiness came from other things and people. When I felt this way, I was often let down and sad because I wasn't happy. It wasn't that those individuals did not love me. It wasn't even that they could not love me. It was that I placed a responsibility and an expectation on them that was never theirs to handle. From that moment on, I chose to make my happiness a priority to me, even if it wasn't a priority to other people. Again, this did not make them bad people, it only showed that my happiness may not have been at the top of their priority list. When my happiness became important to me, I began to walk in the level of truth that I had not walked in before. I recognized that I had the power to be happy all along and I didn't necessarily need an external source to achieve that feeling.

Take today, and spend some time discovering what makes you happy (if you don't already know). This discovery should not be about external things alone. It should also be about things that you provide for yourself. These could be passions or hobbies that you put down years ago that you want to pick back up. You deserve to be happy. Happiness is a possibility; but you must be willing to discover it and find that place every day.

Reflection: When you find your place of happiness nothing and no one can take it away from you. Write an affirmation that speaks to the happiness you desire to have or that you have already found.

_____

_____

_____

_____

_____

_____

_____

Day 18:

How others perceive me doesn't define me,

Have you ever had someone have the wrong perception of you and you didn't know it until after you developed a relationship with them? If you're anything like me, you have experienced people having the wrong perception of who you are or having the wring perception of someone else. People will see you and, without knowing you, they will label you, as "stuck up, arrogant, fake, etc." One thing I dislike about that is that people rarely take the time to build relationships and get to know a person to see if those things are true. Their perception becomes law and that influences how they interact or don't interact with that individual. It even influences how they talk to others about that individual.

Once upon a time I lived to please people. I didn't want anyone to think negatively of me so I did what I could to avoid and prevent that at all costs. What I didn't realize was that I was not being my authentic self. I was wearing masks so frequently that I didn't know who I was. I wanted to be accepted so I became what others expected because I thought that would define me. One of the hardest things for me to do on this journey was find myself. I had to cycle through masks that I wore at church, with my family, with my friends, and my coworkers to find myself. I believed the lie that said that false versions of me were more palatable, but I don't anymore. The truth is that I define myself and the perception of another has no bearing on who I am. I set the bar because I am the bar! Period!

Reflection: I am who I am, and no one gets to choose that for me. Write an affirmation below that highlights your power to be your authentic self.

TAREASHA MON'EA

Day 19:

I am comfortable saying "No," as a complete sentence,

Say this out, loud with me: "NO!" How did that feel? Did you cringe? Did you panic or have a meltdown? Were you excited? No is a word that many of us don't use enough. We become yes women and yes men we create detrimental spaces for ourselves. When this happens, in the words of Beyoncé, "the first time we say no it's like we never said yes." A critical lesson that I've learned in life is that no is a complete sentence, and it doesn't need an explanation. You do not owe anyone an explanation about what you do with your time when you decline something that they ask offer or present to you.

I used to believe the lie that said, my no was only valid when I had something "legitimate" to do. When asked to give or do something, if we have a prior commitment, it takes the pressure off of us when we say no. However, when we are free to be at an event, or to do something that we simply choose not to do, at times it is met with resistance. What you must understand is that you don't owe anyone an explanation for your no. I want you to take some time to practice saying no to things and people. This may not be easy, but it will be worth it, and you will find yourself in a better mental space because of it.

As you are practicing, I want to challenge you not to explain why you can't, or don't want to do something. Let your no be what it is. Although it's only one word, no is a complete sentence. Speak up and protect yourself. Thank me later.

Reflection: Write an affirmation that protects you from feeling guilty when saying no. You don't have to do it just because they ask.

_____

_____

THIS HAS TO BE A LIE…

_____
_____
_____
_____
_____

Day 20:

I will not apologize for being myself.

In my opinion, the worst thing you can apologize for is being yourself. It's the one thing that you will always do so I apologize for it. On this journey, I had to learn that I am who I am, and I will not deny myself to be accepted by anyone or in any space. Now this is not an excuse to demonstrate poor behavior; however, it is an opportunity to validate the person you are in this moment. We live in a day and time where many people find themselves giving half-assed apologies for actions that they're not really sorry for. Their truth is offensive to others, and in some cases, the problem is with the others. People have become so opinionated and entitled that they believe that their thoughts, feelings, and perceptions about the life of another, should cause that other person to change. I've been there before, and that's a place I refuse to return to.

I've come to a place where I cannot apologize for being me. One reason is because no one knows how much and how hard I thought to be here. Accepting my quirks, physical features, the way I think, the way I love, and the way I show up for others took some time. In some areas I'm still evolving and growing, but if I apologize for who I have become I undermine and counteract the work that I have done, I am doing, and will do. I used to believe the lie that there was something wrong with the way I was, so I worked hard to change. Because the change was not sincere, it didn't last long. Now, I make no excuse or apology for who I am. My experiences have shaped me, my faith influences me, and my desires push me. It is my goal to become the best version of myself, but that journey starts with living unapologetically.

Reflection: You don't have to apologize for being who you are. You are all things good even if it's hard to see. Create an affirmation that will help you stand confidently in who you are.

_____

_____

_____

_____

_____

_____

_____

Day 21:

I'm THAT girl!

THAT girl who takes a chance on herself every single day.

THAT girl who is healing, growing, evolving, and becoming the best version of myself.

THAT girl who refuses to give up on herself, her goals or her dreams.

THAT girl who will keep going.

Why am I THAT girl? Well because I made up my mind to be!

Reflection: You are THAT girl. You are THAT guy! Create an affirmation below that states why you are THAT girl or guy.

_____
_____
_____
_____
_____

TAREASHA MON'EA

About the Author

PASSION! If you have ever met or encountered Tareasha Mon'ea, you know almost immediately that she is passionate about everything. Whether it's hosting her own podcast, All Bases Covered – The Podcast, helping her clients tackle administrative tasks as the CEO of ABC Administrative Services, sharing posts on social media, singing karaoke in her parents' backyard or providing a safe space for her family and friends, Tareasha's passion is what most people have come to love about her. Identifying her own struggles with mental health led her on a journey of self-discovery and advocacy for mental and emotional well-being. She whole-heartedly believes that no - thing and no one is worth your peace of mind. Tareasha is a daughter, sister, auntie to 2 amazing young people, and a friend; but most importantly she is an agent of change.

Made in the USA
Columbia, SC
17 July 2023